MAZEL TOV!

IT'S A GIRL

JAMIE KORNGOLD
PHOTOS BY JEFF FINKELSTEIN

KAR-BEN
PUBLISHING

My mommy is having a baby girl.

I go to the hospital to meet my new sister.

Her feet are smaller than mine. Her hands are smaller than mine.

She can't play hopscotch like I can.
She can't even feed herself.

But she is very warm and cuddly. Mommy lets me hold her.

I think she's smiling at me.

When my baby sister is eight days old, we have a special ceremony called a brit bat or simchat bat to welcome her.

My grandparents come all the way from New York with delicious food, including my favorite cookies.

Our family and friends gather.

The cantor leads us in singing Hebrew songs.

My parents announce that my baby sister's name will be Rebecca. She will have a Hebrew name, too.

Rivka bat Avraham v'Yael, Rebecca the daughter of Avraham and Yael. Rivka was the name of my mommy's grandmother. My mommy tells everyone about Great-Grandma Rebecca.

The rabbi blesses my mommy and daddy and the baby.

He has a blessing for me, too.

MAZEL TOV!

IT'S A BOY

JAMIE KORNGOLD
PHOTOS BY JEFF FINKELSTEIN

KAR-BEN
PUBLISHING

To Rebecca, Darren, Lauren and William Payne. — J.K.

To Noah Finkelstein and Daniel Feld who missed their calling. — J.F.

KAR-BEN PUBLISHING
A division of Lerner Publishing Group, Inc.
241 First Avenue North
Minneapolis, MN 55401 USA
1-800-4-KARBEN

Website address: www.karben.com

Main body text set in Shannon Std. 18/26
Typeface provided by Adobe Systems.

Library of Congress Cataloging-in-Publication Data

Korngold, Jamie S.
    [Short stories. Selections]
    Mazel tov! it's a boy ; Mazel tov! it's a girl / by Jamie Korngold ; photographs by Jeff Finkelstein.
        pages   cm
    Titles from separate title pages; works issued back-to-back and inverted.
    Summary: A young Jewish girl and her family welcome a new baby boy with a bris, and in another story, welcome a new baby girl with a brit bat, or naming ceremony.
    ISBN 978–0–4677–1957–5 (lib. bdg. : alk. paper)
    ISBN 978–1–4677–6206–9 (eBook)
    1. Upside-down books—Specimens. [1. Babies—Fiction. 2. Brothers and sisters—Fiction. 3. Sisters—Fiction. 4. Circumcision—Religious aspects—Judaism—Fiction. 5. Brit bat—Fiction. 6. Names, Personal—Fiction. 7. Judaism—Customs and practices—Fiction. 8. Upside-down books. 9. Toy and movable books.] I. Finkelstein, Jeff, illustrator. II. Korngold, Jamie S. Mazel tov! it's a girl. III. Title. IV. Title: Mazel tov! it's a girl.
    PZ7.K83749Maz 2015
    [E]—dc23   2014003607

Manufactured in the United States of America
1 – DP – 12/31/14

My mommy is having a baby. I'm going to be a big sister.

It's a boy! I'm so glad to finally meet him.

I've been waiting to play with him.

He sure sleeps a lot. But he's very cute.

I wonder when he'll be big enough to play soccer with me.

When my baby brother is eight days old, we have a ceremony called a bris or brit milah to welcome him.

My saba and savta come all the way from Israel. They bring a kippah for the baby and a Kiddush cup for me.

9

Rabbi Rubenstein, who is a mohel, recites a blessing. Then my parents announce my brother's name. He has both a Hebrew name and an English name, just like I do.

His Hebrew name is David Ben Avraham v'Yael, David the son of Avraham and Yael. David is named after Daddy's Uncle David who was a brave and kind man. We hope our David will be brave and kind, too.

I stand under a tallit with my parents and new baby brother.

The rabbi says a blessing for the whole family including me. Then it is time to celebrate.

13

My daddy sings the blessing over wine. He puts some on a little piece of gauze and gives it to David to taste. Daddy pours grape juice in my new kiddush cup.

All the children are invited to bless the challah.
David is too little to have a taste.

We eat sweets in the hope that our baby's life will be sweet.

I am so happy to be a big sister.